Different

By

Geoffrey Samuel Keith

*To my wife Kristy and my children Leia and Levi.
Life is full of so many moments and all of my
favorite ones are with you.*

EMILY'S
ENTOURAGE

Every day I wake up and look in the mirror. And each time I do, a spot does appear.

It's on my nose right in the middle of my face. When I go to school I couldn't feel more out of place.

I look around at everyone else and as far as I see, not one person at school has a birthmark like me.

I wish things were different and I could easily blend. Maybe there's a school for kids with birthmarks I could attend.

I feel so different because no one looks like I do. If I just looked normal, I could start anew.

I walked around with my head held low. Hoping no one would see, no one would know.

This is the way that I used to feel. Until I met some friends who helped me deal.

One day at school I was approached by a group who said, "Hey, Leia, we like you, here is the scoop."

One by one they started to talk. And with every word, I was in shock.

"My name is Laura and I'm really lanky."

"My name is Sick Henry so I carry this hanky."

"My name is Tommy and I weigh too much."

"My name is Tammy and I walk with a crutch."

Laura

Henry

Tommy

Tammy

"Hi, I'm Lisa and my eyes are too close."

"Hi, I'm Brian, I'm told my breath smells pretty gross."

"Hey there, I'm Larry and I'm kinda hairy."

"My friends call me Fritz and I have lots of zits."

Everyone has something that they may want to fix. That's what makes life interesting, we're all a huge mix.

We think your birthmark is different, but also really neat. That's why we came over so we could finally meet...

If you want to join us we'd love for you to be a part of our squad."

I couldn't believe it, this must be an act from God.

"Yes, of course, that sounds really fun!" I answered them all.

And then stinky Brian kicked me a red ball.

It was such a great day, I made so many friends. It goes to show that you never know how each story ends.

I realize now people are different all over the place, I just happen to have a difference right on my face.

I used to be sad about this spot on my nose. But my birthmark's my trademark one could suppose.

I love that I'm different, I love being me. You're different too, that's how it should be.

THE END

Made in the USA
Columbia, SC
09 November 2024

45888991R00018